The Complete
Disciple of Christ
Guidebook

By Karajah Yashar

BLACKSTONE
PUBLISHING

Orlando, FL 2024

www.bspbooks.com

ISBN: 978-1-962691-34-5

First Edition: August 2024

Table of Contents

Introduction: What is a Disciple

Being a disciple of Christ means committing oneself to follow Jesus' teachings, emulate His life, and participate in His mission. This commitment involves a deep, personal relationship with Jesus, grounded in faith and love. Discipleship is not merely about adhering to a set of doctrines or religious practices but about a transformative journey of becoming more like Christ. It requires a willingness to surrender one's own desires and priorities in favor of God's will, as Jesus stated in Matthew 16:24 (KJV): "If any man will come after me, let him deny himself, and take up his cross, and follow me." This self-denial and carrying of the cross symbolize the readiness to face hardships, make sacrifices, and pursue righteousness in a world often contrary to Christ's values.

Additionally, being a disciple means engaging actively in Jesus' mission of spreading the gospel and serving others. It is about living out the Great Commission found in Matthew 28:19-20 (KJV): "Go ye therefore, and teach all nations, baptizing them in the name of the Father, and of the Son, and of the Holy Ghost: Teaching them to observe all things whatsoever I have commanded you." Discipleship involves evangelism, teaching, and demonstrating God's love through acts of service and compassion. It is about building and nurturing a community of disciples, supporting one another in faith, and working collectively to advance God's kingdom on earth. This holistic approach to discipleship emphasizes not only personal spiritual growth but also the responsibility to impact the world positively by reflecting Christ's love and truth in everyday life.

The Tenets of Discipleship

A Disciple follows in the complete Way, Truth, and Life of Jesus Christ, striving to emulate His example in every aspect of their lives. This involves recognizing and adhering to several fundamental assertions. First, the Incarnation: the belief that Jesus Christ is the Son of God who took on human flesh (John 1:14). This foundational belief underscores the divine nature of Jesus and His mission to bring humanity back into a relationship with God.

A Disciple of Christ is dedicated to following the Life and Ministry of Jesus, as depicted in the Gospels. This includes His teachings, miracles, and the example He set during His life on earth (Matthew 5-7, Luke 4:18-19). Disciples commit to living out Jesus' teachings in their daily lives, embodying His principles of love, compassion, humility, and obedience to God's will. The Crucifixion, where Jesus sacrificed His life on the cross for the sins of humanity (Matthew 27:32-56, John 19:16-37), is central to a disciple's faith. They acknowledge the significance of this act of love and redemption and seek to live in a way that honors Jesus' sacrifice.

The Resurrection, where Jesus rose from the dead on the third day, demonstrating His victory over sin and death (Matthew 28:1-10, Luke 24:1-12), is another core belief for a Disciple. This event affirms Jesus' divinity and the truth of His message, offering disciples the hope of eternal life and a restored relationship with God. The Ascension of Jesus into heaven is also significant, as it represents His exaltation and the promise of His return. Disciples of Christ also follow God's laws and commandments under the New Covenant, including dietary laws, High Holy days, Sabbaths, and moral laws such as not lying, stealing, or committing adultery.

Disciple of Christ vs Christianity

The difference between a Disciple of Christ and a Christian often lies in the depth of commitment and adherence to the teachings and example of Jesus. While someone who identifies as a Christian can be a Disciple of Christ, not all Christians are disciples in the full sense. Many Christians follow the traditions of man, such as celebrating holidays like Christmas, Easter, and Halloween, which have pagan origins. They often disregard dietary laws and other commandments, believing that everything is clean and permissible. However, Christ emphasized in Matthew 5:17-19 that He did not come to abolish the law but to fulfill it. A Disciple puts the ways of Christ before the traditions of the world, seeking to live in accordance with God's laws and Jesus' example, demonstrating a deeper commitment to their faith.

The Term Disciple vs Christian

The early church did not originally refer to themselves as Christians; this term was actually a mocking name given to them by others. According to Acts 11:26, "The disciples were called Christians first in Antioch." The term "Christian" was initially used by outsiders as a derogatory label to mock those who followed Jesus Christ. It was not a name that the early disciples chose for themselves. Instead, they identified as disciples, a term that emphasizes their commitment to learning from and emulating Jesus in their daily lives.

Jesus Himself referred to His followers as disciples and explicitly instructed them to go and make disciples of all nations. In Matthew 28:19-20, Jesus commands, "Go therefore and make disciples of all nations, baptizing them in the name of the Father and of the Son and of the Holy Spirit, teaching them to observe all that I have commanded you." This commission highlights the importance of discipleship—being a student and follower of Jesus' teachings and example. The term "disciple" carries a deeper connotation of ongoing learning, commitment, and transformation, which was central to the identity of the early disciples.

The shift from being known as disciples to being labeled as Christians marked a significant change in the identity and perception of Jesus' followers. While the name "Christian" eventually became a widely accepted and embraced term, its origins as a term of mockery underscore the challenges and opposition faced by the early church. Despite this, the early disciples remained steadfast in their mission to spread Jesus' teachings and to make disciples, as He had instructed them. Their primary focus was on living out their faith authentically and faithfully, following the example set by Jesus Christ.

Chapter 1: The Old Testament Foundation

The Old Testament, often referred to as the Hebrew Bible, is fundamental to understanding the New Covenant established in the New Testament. The teachings, laws, statutes, and commandments found within the Old Testament provide a crucial foundation for the life of a disciple. Without an in-depth understanding of these scriptures, the New Testament can be misunderstood and taken out of context. When the Apostle Paul admonished disciples to "study to show thyself approved" (2 Timothy 2:15), the New Testament as we know it had not yet been compiled. Paul was referring to the Old Testament writings, emphasizing their enduring importance and relevance.

Paul himself, a learned Pharisee before his conversion to becoming a disciple, deeply respected the Old Testament. He called it our "schoolmaster" leading us unto Christ (Galatians 3:24). This metaphor underscores the idea that the Old Testament provides foundational lessons necessary for understanding and embracing the teachings of Jesus. Just as we do not discard everything we learned in school after graduation, disciples should not disregard the Old Testament after accepting the New Covenant. The principles, values, and instructions contained within the Old Testament are essential for shaping a disciple's life and faith.

The Old Testament teaches various aspects of living according to God's will. It encompasses moral laws, social laws, and dietary laws, all designed to guide God's people in proper living. The moral laws, such as the Ten Commandments, lay the groundwork for ethical behavior and justice. These commandments are timeless, reflecting God's character and expectations for humanity. Social laws provide guidance on how to live harmoniously within a community, emphasizing fairness, compassion, and respect for others. Dietary laws, while often overlooked, teach discipline and mindfulness in what we consume, reminding us that our bodies are temples of God.

One of the significant shifts from the Old Testament to the New Testament is the law of sacrifice. Under the Old Covenant, the sacrificial system involved offering animals, such as lambs and rams, to atone for sins. These sacrifices were imperfect and temporary, pointing forward to the ultimate sacrifice. With the advent of Jesus Christ, the Lamb of God, the sacrificial system was fulfilled. His death on the cross provided the perfect and final atonement for sin, rendering the old sacrificial practices obsolete. However, this does not mean that all Old Testament laws were abolished.

Many Christians today mistakenly believe that the entire Old Testament law was done away with by the New Covenant. However, a closer examination of Paul's teachings reveals that he specifically referred to the law of sacrifice being fulfilled in Christ. The moral, social, and dietary laws remain significant. God called these laws and High Holy Days a perpetual covenant, signifying their everlasting importance and relevance. These instructions were meant to guide His people in holy living and worship. The term "perpetual covenant" underscores the timeless nature of these commandments, indicating they are to be observed and honored for all generations. They continue to guide disciples in righteous living and reflect the enduring principles of God's kingdom. Observing the Feast days, Sabbaths, and New Moons remain important, as these observances help disciples to remember and celebrate God's actions throughout history and in their own lives.

When the Apostle Paul advises not to judge people regarding new moons and Sabbaths (Colossians 2:16-17), he is not advocating for the abandonment of these observances. Paul himself is documented as keeping the Sabbath, demonstrating its continued significance in his life (Acts 17:2, Acts 18:4). His message focuses on avoiding legalistic and overly critical attitudes toward how others observe these days. Paul emphasizes the spirit of the law rather than rigid adherence to human traditions, encouraging disciples to honor these holy days in a way that reflects their faith and devotion without falling into the trap of judgmentalism.

Christ similarly addressed the hypocrisy of the Pharisees concerning the Sabbath, underscoring that "the Sabbath was made for man, not man for the Sabbath" (Mark 2:27). Jesus highlighted the importance of mercy and the well-being of individuals over strict nit picking of Sabbath rules. He condemned the Pharisees for their focus on minute regulations while neglecting the broader purpose of the Sabbath, which is to provide rest and spiritual renewal. Both Jesus and Paul call for a balanced approach, encouraging disciples to observe the Sabbath and other holy days meaningfully and sincerely, without becoming entangled in judgment or legalism.

The Old Testament is indispensable for understanding the New Covenant and living as a disciple of Christ. It provides the essential foundation upon which the teachings of Jesus and the apostles are built. By studying the Old Testament, disciples can better understand God's mind and and become reflective of His eternal truths. The transition from the Old to the New Covenant does not nullify the former but fulfills and amplifies it, showing the continuity of God's plan for humanity. Thus, the Old Testament remains a vital part of faith and practice, guiding disciples in their journey of righteous living.

Chapter 2: The Incarnation of Christ

The Gospel Begins with the Incarnation

The story of the gospel begins with a profound and mysterious event: the incarnation. The term "incarnation" refers to the knowledge and faith that Jesus Christ, the eternal Son of God, took on human flesh. This foundational truth is beautifully expressed in John 1:14, which states, "The Word became flesh and made his dwelling among us." This single verse encapsulates the essence of the incarnation, highlighting the divine decision to become intimately involved in the human experience.

The Word Became Flesh

God's laws have been in existence since the very beginning of creation, serving as the foundation upon which the universe was established. In the book of Genesis, when God declared, "Let there be light," He was not referring to the physical light of the sun, moon, or stars, which were not created until the fourth day of creation (Genesis 1:14-16). Instead, this command signified the introduction of divine order and law into the cosmos. This primordial light represents God's presence and the moral and natural laws that govern all creation. Proverbs 6:23 states "For the commandment is a lamp; and the law is light; and reproofs of instruction are the way of life". Initially, humanity was expected to understand and adhere to these laws directly from God the Father, without the need for written instruction.

Recognizing the need for a more concrete expression of His laws, God provided the written law to His people. This began with the Torah, delivered through Moses, which contained commandments and guidelines for living a life pleasing to God. The writings of the prophets further elaborated on these laws, offering guidance, warnings, and promises. Despite this, God's people struggled to faithfully keep the law, often misunderstanding or disregarding its deeper spiritual significance. Observing their continual shortcomings, God saw fit to send the ultimate revelation of His law: the Word made flesh, Jesus Christ. Christ became the light of the world, as He proclaimed in John 8:12: "I am the light of the world: he that followeth me shall not walk in darkness, but shall have the light of life."

Jesus' arrival did not signify the abolition of the law but rather its fulfillment. As stated in Matthew 5:17, Christ came to fulfill the law, providing a perfect example of how to live in accordance with God's will. Through His life, teachings, and sacrificial death, Jesus embodied the true essence of the law, demonstrating love, mercy, and justice. In fulfilling the law, He revealed its full meaning and intent, guiding disciples on how to genuinely keep and live by God's commandments. Thus, through the incarnation of the Word, God not only clarified His expectations but also empowered His people to achieve the righteousness that the law demands.

The incarnation is not merely an abstract doctrine but a transformative reality. It bridges the chasm between the divine and the human, making it possible for people to relate to God in a personal and tangible way. In Jesus, the abstract becomes concrete, the invisible becomes visible, and the transcendent becomes immanent. He is Emmanuel, "God with us" (Matthew 1:23), demonstrating that God is not distant but intimately involved in the world.

A Fulfillment of the Old Covenant

To fully appreciate the incarnation, it is essential to understand it in the context of the Old Covenant. Under the Old Covenant, the Israelites had the written law, the Word of God, as revealed through the prophets and the Scriptures. This law was a guide to living in accordance with God's will but was often seen as distant and challenging to fulfill. The Word was external, written on tablets of stone.

In the incarnation, the Word became flesh. Jesus Christ embodied the law and showed humanity how to live it out. By living a perfect life of obedience, love, and compassion, Jesus provided a living, breathing example of what it means to live according to God's Word. His life was a testament to the law's true purpose: to guide people into a loving relationship with God and each other.

The Testimony of Heaven

The significance of the incarnation is further underscored by the testimony of heaven. In 1 John 5:7, it is written, "For there are three that bear record in heaven, the Father, the Word, and the Holy Spirit: and these three are one." This verse highlights the unity and harmony within the Trinity concerning the incarnation. The Father sent the written Word, then the Son, into the world. The Holy Spirit was then given after Christ's ascension to bear witness to this truth. Both the Torah and Christ's ascension occurred during the High Holy day of Feast of Weeks or Pentecost. This divine testimony affirms the centrality of the incarnation in God's plan of salvation.

Confessing Jesus Came in the Flesh

Acknowledging the incarnation is crucial for anyone seeking to live as a disciple of Jesus Christ, as it affirms the belief that God entered human history in the person of Jesus to provide a perfect example of righteous living. This recognition not only grounds one's faith in the reality of Jesus' humanity and divinity but also inspires a deeper commitment to following His teachings and emulating His life. In 1 John 4:2-3, it is written,

"This is how you can recognize the Spirit of God: Every spirit that acknowledges that Jesus Christ has come in the flesh is from God, but every spirit that does not acknowledge Jesus is not from God."

This passage emphasizes that confessing Jesus Christ came in the flesh is a fundamental aspect of being a disciple of Christ. It is a declaration of belief in the reality of the incarnation and the profound implications it has for salvation and discipleship.

The First Step in Discipleship

The first step to living as a disciple of Jesus is to acknowledge that Jesus Christ walked the earth. This acknowledgment is not merely intellectual assent but a heartfelt acceptance of the truth of the incarnation. It means recognizing Jesus as the Son of God who became human, lived a sinless life, died for our sins, and rose again. It involves understanding that Jesus is not just a historical figure but the living Word of God who reveals the Father to us.

By embracing the incarnation, disciples are invited into a deeper relationship with God. They are called to follow Jesus' example, to live out the Word in their daily lives, and to reflect the love, grace, and truth that He embodied. The incarnation is the foundation upon which discipleship is built, calling disciples to live in the light of the reality that God sent His Son to redeem humanity.

Supposition

The incarnation is the bedrock of the gospel message. It signifies God's profound commitment to humanity by bridging the divine and human divide. By becoming flesh, Jesus provided a tangible example of how to live out the Word of God. Confessing that Jesus came in the flesh is essential for authentic discipleship. As disciples embrace the truth of the incarnation, they are called to live in a manner that reflects the love and grace of the Word made flesh, Jesus Christ.

Chapter 3: The Life and Ministry of Jesus

Jesus' Life and Ministry

The life and ministry of Jesus Christ are pivotal to the gospel narrative, providing a blueprint for righteous living and revealing the nature of God's kingdom. Through His teachings, miracles, and personal example, Jesus set the standard for how His followers are to live. His ethical teachings, most notably encapsulated in the Sermon on the Mount (Matthew 5-7), lay out principles of humility, mercy, and love that challenge and inspire disciples to higher moral standards. Additionally, His miracles, such as healing the sick and raising the dead, demonstrated His divine authority and compassion, confirming His message and mission (Luke 4:18-19).

The Sermon on the Mount

The Sermon on the Mount is a central component of Jesus' teachings, offering profound insights into God's expectations for human behavior. Found in Matthew 5-7, this sermon addresses a wide range of ethical issues, including anger, lust, divorce, oaths, retaliation, and love for enemies. Jesus emphasizes the importance of internal righteousness over external compliance, urging His followers to seek purity of heart and genuine piety. The Beatitudes, which open the sermon, describe the blessings associated with attitudes such as meekness, mercy, and peacemaking, highlighting the values of the kingdom of God.

One key lesson from the Sermon on the Mount is the call to internal righteousness over external compliance. Jesus challenges traditional interpretations of the Law by emphasizing the importance of inner transformation and purity of heart. For example, He teaches that anger and lust are as sinful as murder and adultery, respectively, because they stem from a heart that is not aligned with God's will. This lesson underscores the need for disciples to cultivate an inner life that reflects God's values, going beyond mere outward observance of religious practices.

Another significant lesson from the Sermon on the Mount is the call to radical love and mercy. Jesus instructs His followers to love their enemies, bless those who curse them, and pray for those who persecute them (Matthew 5:44). This teaching turns conventional wisdom on its head, advocating for a love that transcends natural inclinations and mirrors the unconditional love of God. By calling His followers to such a high standard of love, Jesus sets the expectation that His disciples should extend grace and compassion even to those who may seem undeserving.

Additionally, the Beatitudes highlight the blessedness of traits such as meekness, mercy, and peacemaking, encouraging disciples to embody these qualities in their daily lives. These lessons collectively paint a picture of a countercultural kingdom where humility, compassion, and love are paramount. They challenge disciples to live out these values in a world often marked by self-interest and division, promoting a lifestyle that reflects the heart of God's kingdom. The Sermon on the Mount, therefore, serves as a comprehensive guide for ethical and spiritual living, urging disciples to internalize and practice the teachings of Jesus.

Miracles and Divine Authority

Jesus' miracles serve as powerful testimonies to His divine authority and compassion. Through acts of healing, exorcisms, and even raising the dead, Jesus manifested God's power and mercy in tangible ways. These miracles were not merely displays of supernatural power but were deeply connected to His message of the kingdom of God. Each miracle demonstrated that God's reign had broken into the present world, offering glimpses of the restoration and wholeness that God's kingdom brings. By performing these acts, Jesus revealed the transformative impact of divine intervention in a world marred by sin and suffering.

These miracles illustrated the compassionate nature of Jesus' ministry. He healed the sick, restored sight to the blind, cleansed lepers, and cast out demons, showing His deep concern for the physical and spiritual well-being of individuals. The miracles were expressions of God's love and mercy, addressing both immediate needs and deeper, long-term restoration. Jesus' willingness to touch the untouchable and heal the marginalized demonstrated that the kingdom of God was inclusive, accessible, and transformative for all who would come to Him in faith.

Furthermore, each miracle served as a sign pointing to Jesus as the Messiah, inviting people to faith and repentance. The miraculous acts were not ends in themselves but were meant to lead people to recognize Jesus' divine identity and mission. They authenticated His claims and teachings, compelling observers to confront the reality of God's presence among them. As people witnessed these miracles, they were invited to believe in Jesus, repent of their sins, and embrace the new life He offered. In this way, Jesus' miracles were integral to His ministry, reinforcing His message and drawing people into a deeper relationship with God.

The Kingdom of God and Repentance

Central to Jesus' ministry was the proclamation of the kingdom of God. His primary message to His disciples was,

"Repent, for the kingdom of heaven is at hand"
(Matthew 4:17).

Repentance, as taught by Jesus, involves a profound turning away from sin, which is defined as transgression of God's laws. As 1 John 3:4 states, "Whosoever committeth sin transgresseth also the law: for sin is the transgression of the law." This biblical definition underscores that sin is not merely a matter of personal failure but a violation of God's established commandments. Jesus' call to repentance is therefore a call to realign one's life with God's will, to abandon behaviors and practices that contravene His laws, and to embrace a lifestyle that reflects His righteous standards.

This call to repentance is not merely an abstract spiritual concept but has practical implications for daily living. Many people today break God's laws in various ways, such as lying, committing adultery, not honoring their parents, breaking the Sabbath, disregarding dietary laws, and stealing. Jesus never stated that these laws were abolished. Instead, He emphasized their continued relevance and the need for His followers to live in accordance with them. By turning from these sinful behaviors and aligning their lives with God's commandments, individuals can begin to experience the transformative power of the kingdom of God in their lives here on earth.

Repentance, therefore, is both a personal and communal journey back to God's ways. It involves a heartfelt acknowledgment of one's sins, a sincere turning away from them, and a committed effort to follow God's laws. As individuals embrace this process, they open themselves to the blessings of the kingdom of God, experiencing its peace, justice, and righteousness in their lives. Jesus' message of repentance is a timeless call that invites everyone to restore their relationship with God, live in harmony with His commandments, and reflect His kingdom values in every aspect of their lives.

The Kingdom of God and Eternity

Jesus taught that the kingdom of God is not merely a future reality but also a present experience. This teaching is pivotal because it redefines the relationship between disciples and the divine, bringing the reality of God's reign into the here and now. Jesus explained that eternity, which has no beginning or end, is ever-present and accessible. By living in accordance with God's laws and embodying the values of the kingdom, such as love, justice, mercy, and humility, disciples can experience a taste of heaven on earth. This understanding invites disciples to live out the principles of the kingdom daily, fostering a life that reflects God's eternal presence.

Moreover, Jesus' declaration that the kingdom of God is within us (Luke 17:21) suggests that God's presence and reign are intimately accessible to each disciple. This internalization of the kingdom challenges the notion that God is distant or confined to the heavens. Instead, it emphasizes the immanence of God in the lives of His disciples. By recognizing that the kingdom is within, disciples are encouraged to seek spiritual growth and transformation from within, allowing God's will to guide their thoughts, actions, and decisions. This perspective nurtures a profound sense of connection and personal responsibility in living out the faith.

This teaching profoundly impacts the daily life and spirituality of disciples. It means that experiencing God's kingdom is not limited to a distant, future hope but is an immediate reality that can influence and shape the present. By embracing this truth, disciples are empowered to make meaningful changes in their lives and communities, reflecting the kingdom's values in tangible ways. This approach fosters a dynamic faith that seeks to manifest God's love and justice in the world, demonstrating that the kingdom of God is not only a future promise but a present reality actively transforming lives and societies.

Faith and Works

Faith and works are inseparable components of genuine living for a disciple. Many people mistakenly believe that faith alone is sufficient for salvation, thinking that merely believing in Jesus Christ guarantees their place in heaven. Jesus Himself actually refutes this notion. In Matthew 7:21 He states, "Not every one that saith unto me, Lord, Lord, shall enter into the kingdom of heaven; but he that doeth the will of my Father which is in heaven." This clearly shows that faith must be accompanied by action—specifically, doing God's will—to enter the kingdom of heaven. Faith is foundational, but it must be lived out through our actions and obedience to God's commands.

Unfortunately, many pastors propagate the doctrine of faith alone as sufficient for salvation, which is a partial truth that can mislead disciples. The book of James directly addresses this issue, stating in James 2:26 , "For as the body without the spirit is dead, so faith without works is dead also." This verse emphasizes that faith without corresponding actions is lifeless and ineffective. Therefore, preaching that faith alone is enough without encouraging disciples to live out their faith through works is promoting a dead doctrine. Genuine faith inevitably produces good works, reflecting the transformative power of the gospel in a disciple's life.

The Apostle Paul also underscores the importance of upholding the law through faith. In Romans 3:31 he writes, "Do we then make void the law through faith? God forbid: yea, we establish the law." Paul asserts that faith does not nullify the law but rather upholds it. True faith leads disciples to live in accordance with God's laws, embodying His righteousness in their daily lives. This harmonious relationship between faith and works demonstrates a comprehensive understanding of salvation that aligns with biblical teaching, rejecting any notion that faith alone suffices without the evidence of good works.

Moreover, the idea that mere belief ensures salvation is further challenged by the requirement for perseverance. The Bible emphasizes that enduring in faith and works throughout one's lifetime is essential. In Matthew 24:13, Jesus says, "But he that shall endure unto the end, the same shall be saved." This underscores that salvation is not a one-time event but a lifelong journey of faithfulness and obedience.

Disciples must continually strive to live according to God's will, demonstrating their faith through their actions until the end. This enduring commitment reflects the true essence of being a disciple of Christ, where faith and works are intertwined in the pursuit of eternal life.

Mission to the Lost Sheep

Jesus' ministry initially focused on the "lost sheep of the house of Israel", reflecting His mission to address the spiritual and social needs of His own people. "These twelve Jesus sent forth, and commanded them, saying, Go not into the way of the Gentiles, and into any city of the Samaritans enter ye not: but go rather to the lost sheep of the house of Israel. And as ye go, preach, saying, The kingdom of heaven is at hand" (Matthew 10:5-7). He directed His disciples to prioritize these lost sheep, who had strayed from God's ways and lost their true identity. This mission was rooted in a desire to restore their relationship with God and reinstate their understanding of His laws. Jesus' approach was both a call to repentance and a reaffirmation of their covenant with God, highlighting the importance of reclaiming their identity as God's chosen people and returning to a life aligned with His commandments.

The historical context of Israel's captivity, especially the American captivity via the Trans-Atlantic slave trade, has played a significant role in this loss of identity. "And the LORD shall bring thee into Egypt again with ships, by the way whereof I spake unto thee, Thou shalt see it no more again: and there ye shall be sold unto your enemies for bondmen and bondwomen, and no man shall buy you" (Deuteronomy 28:68). Many Israelites, scattered and subjected to various forms of oppression and cultural assimilation, have forgotten their heritage and strayed from the laws given by God. This loss of identity has led to widespread struggles, including social, economic, and spiritual challenges. By reaching out to the lost sheep, Jesus aimed to heal these fractures, offering a pathway back to God and a restoration of their true identity. His ministry underscored the importance of knowing one's heritage and living in accordance with God's laws as a foundation for individual and communal well-being.

Today, this mission remains relevant as many Israelites in America and beyond continue to live without a full knowledge of their identity or a commitment to the way of Christ. Often labeled with various bywords rather than being recognized as Israel, these lost sheep navigate life disconnected from their spiritual roots and divine purpose. "And thou shalt become an astonishment, a proverb, and a byword, among all nations whither the LORD shall lead thee" (Deuteronomy 28:27). Many people have a false idea about who the Jews are and the real Israelites. As Revelation 3:9 states, "Behold, I will make them of the synagogue of Satan, which say they are Jews, and are not, but do lie." Understanding the true identity of the Israelites is essential for comprehending biblical prophecies and teachings accurately. Jesus' call to the lost sheep is a reminder of the ongoing need to reach out to those who have lost their way, offering them the hope and direction found in reclaiming their identity and returning to God's laws. This mission encourages modern disciples to actively engage in restoring and supporting these individuals, helping them to rediscover their place in God's plan and live in accordance with His teachings.

The Great Commission

After His resurrection and before His ascension, Jesus expanded His mission, instructing His disciples to go to all nations and teach the gospel. "Go ye therefore, and teach all nations, baptizing them in the name of the Father, and of the Son, and of the Holy Ghost: Teaching them to observe all things whatsoever I have commanded you: and, lo, I am with you alway, even unto the end of the world. Amen" (Matthew 28:19-20). This Great Commission extended the reach of the gospel beyond the house of Israel to include Gentiles, meaning all other nations. The apostle Paul reiterated this mission, emphasizing the need to reach both Hebrews and Gentiles with the message of salvation. Disciples are tasked with teaching people how to follow God's law as Jesus did, embodying the principles He taught and living out the values of the kingdom. "After this I beheld, and, lo, a great multitude, which no man could number, of all nations, and kindreds, and people, and tongues, stood before the throne, and before the Lamb, clothed with white robes, and palms in their hands; And cried with a loud voice, saying, Salvation to our God which sitteth upon the throne, and unto the Lamb" (Revelation 7:9-10).

The life and ministry of Jesus Christ are central to understanding the gospel. Through His teachings, miracles, and example, Jesus revealed the nature of God's kingdom and set a standard for righteous living. His call to repentance and His teaching on the kingdom of God invite disciples to experience God's reign in the present and to live in accordance with His laws. By reaching out to the lost sheep and commissioning His disciples to go to all nations, Jesus ensured that the message of the gospel would spread throughout the world, offering hope and salvation to all who believe.

Chapter 4: The Crucifixion

The Significance of the Crucifixion

Central to the gospel narrative is the crucifixion of Jesus Christ, an event that stands as the ultimate demonstration of God's sacrificial love and the profound seriousness of sin. The Gospels vividly depict this event, detailing how Jesus was condemned, mocked, and ultimately nailed to a cross to die (Matthew 27:32-56, John 19:16-37). This brutal and unjust execution was not merely a tragic end to a good man's life but the fulfillment of a divine plan for the redemption of humanity. Jesus' willingness to endure such suffering underscores the depth of God's love for the world and His commitment to save it from the consequences of sin.

The crucifixion highlights the gravity of sin and the necessity of a perfect sacrifice to atone for it. Sin, defined as the transgression of God's law, creates a separation between humanity and God that cannot be bridged without repentance. Jesus, the sinless Son of God, took upon Himself the weight of humanity's sins, offering His life as a ransom to reconcile humanity with

God. His death on the cross satisfied the demands of divine justice, making it possible for people to receive forgiveness and be restored to a right relationship with God. This act of atonement emphasizes that sin is not a trivial matter but one that required an extraordinary sacrifice.

Moreover, the crucifixion serves as the ultimate expression of God's love for humanity. By willingly enduring the cross, Jesus demonstrated that there is no limit to God's love and mercy. John 3:16 encapsulates this truth: "For God so loved the world that He gave His one and only Son, that whoever believes in Him shall not perish but have eternal life." Jesus' sacrificial death was a deliberate act to provide a path to salvation for all who believe. This profound expression of love calls disciples to respond with faith, gratitude, and a commitment to live in accordance with God's will. The crucifixion, therefore, is not only a historical event but a transformative truth that continues to inspire and guide the lives of disciples.

The New Covenant

Jesus' crucifixion occurred during the week of Passover and the Feast of Unleavened Bread, a time rich in Israelite symbolism and significance. The Passover commemorates Israel's deliverance from Egyptian bondage, marked by the sacrifice of a lamb whose blood spared the Israelites from death (Exodus 12:1-14). By being crucified during this pivotal week, God positioned Hims as the fulfillment of the Passover lamb, signifying a new deliverance — not from physical bondage, but from the bondage of sin. This parallel is further emphasized in 1 Corinthians 5:7, where the Apostle Paul declares, "For Christ, our Passover lamb, has been sacrificed."

In this context, Jesus' death marked the establishment of a new covenant, as He declared at the Last Supper, "This cup is the new covenant in my blood, which is poured out for you" (Luke 22:20). The old covenant, characterized by the sacrificial system of lambs, goats, and rams for atonement of sins, was brought to its fulfillment and completion in Jesus' perfect sacrifice. The Apostle Paul elucidates this transition in Hebrews 10:10, stating, "We have been made holy through the sacrifice of the body of Jesus Christ once for all." This new covenant underscores a shift from repetitive animal sacrifices to a singular, all-sufficient sacrifice in Jesus Christ.

It is the Passover, not Easter, that truly commemorates the crucifixion of Jesus Christ. The observance of Passover aligns with the biblical narrative, marking the time when Jesus, our Passover Lamb, was sacrificed for the sins of humanity. In contrast, Easter has origins rooted in ancient pagan festivals honoring the goddess Eostre. It celebrated spring and fertility with bunny and egg symbolism. This was later integrated into Christian traditions. Recognizing the Passover as the commemoration of Jesus' crucifixion honors the historical and spiritual significance of His sacrifice, aligning with the scriptural accounts and the early disciples practice of observing His death and resurrection during the Passover season.

The Law of Sacrifice

Many mistakenly believe that Jesus' crucifixion did away with the entire Mosaic Law, but a closer examination of Scripture reveals that it was specifically the sacrificial aspect of the law that was fulfilled and replaced. The ceremonial laws regarding sacrifices were no longer necessary because Jesus, as the perfect and ultimate sacrifice, fulfilled their purpose. The Apostle Paul clarifies this in Colossians 2:14, where he speaks of the written code with its regulations being nailed to the cross, indicating the end of the sacrificial system. However, the moral and ethical teachings of the law remain relevant and continue to guide Christ's disciples.

Instead of the old sacrificial system, disciples now observe Communion, also known as the Lord's Supper, as instituted by Jesus. During Communion, disciples partake of unleavened bread and wine or grape juice, symbolizing Jesus' body and blood, in remembrance of His sacrifice (1 Corinthians 11:23-26). This practice serves as a continual reminder of the new covenant and the disciple's relationship with Christ. It signifies the shift from the old covenant rituals to a new, more intimate form of worship and remembrance. Through Communion, disciples are called to reflect on Jesus' sacrifice, reaffirm their faith, and commit to living in accordance with His teachings.

The Gravity of Sin

The crucifixion of Jesus Christ starkly highlights the gravity of sin and its devastating effects on humanity. Sin, defined in the Bible as the transgression of God's law, creates a profound separation between people and God, leading to spiritual death and eternal separation from Him. This separation is not merely a temporary state but a condition with eternal consequences, emphasizing the seriousness of sin. The horrific nature of Jesus' death on the cross serves as a stark reminder of the severity of sin and the just penalty it incurs. This brutal execution underscores that sin is not a trivial matter but a grave offense against a holy God that necessitates a profound and costly remedy.

By taking upon Himself the sins of the world, Jesus bore the punishment that humanity deserved, thus satisfying the demands of divine justice. His suffering and death were necessary to atone for sin, bridging the gap between a holy God and fallen humanity. This act of atonement is foundational to the disciples of Christ, highlighting that only through Jesus' sacrificial death can reconciliation with God be achieved. The cross represents both the seriousness of sin and the depths of God's love, as He provided a means for humanity's redemption. This profound truth calls disciples to a deeper appreciation of Jesus' sacrifice and a commitment to living in a way that honors the price He paid.

The Biblical High Holy Day of Atonement, which used to be marked by animal sacrifices, is now observed as a day of fasting and communion, reflecting the sacrifice of Jesus. Jesus is regarded as the ultimate High Priest, whose once-for-all sacrifice surpasses and fulfills the old sacrificial system. Other communions of the body and blood of Jesus occur during the Sabbaths, New Moons, High Holy Days, and special ceremonies such as confessions and guilt offerings. These observances are significant moments of reflection and spiritual renewal for disciples, reinforcing the centrality of Jesus' sacrifice in their faith. Through these practices, disciples continually remember and honor the atonement provided by Jesus, allowing it to shape their worship and daily lives.

The Extent of God's Love

The crucifixion powerfully illustrates the extent of God's love for humanity. Jesus' voluntary sacrifice was the ultimate act of love, as He laid down His life to save others. John 3:16 encapsulates this profound truth: "For God so loved the world that He gave His one and only Son, that whoever believes in Him shall not perish but have eternal life." This verse underscores the magnitude of God's love, revealing that He was willing to offer His beloved Son to endure immense suffering and death for the sake of humanity's redemption. Jesus' death was not an accident or merely the result of human schemes; it was a deliberate act of divine love and mercy, planned from the foundation of the world to provide a path to salvation.

Through His death, Jesus demonstrated that there is no limit to God's love and no length to which He will not go to redeem His creation. The crucifixion stands as a testament to the sacrificial nature of God's love, showing that He values humanity so deeply that He was willing to endure the ultimate sacrifice to restore the broken relationship caused by sin. This act of divine love invites disciples to respond with faith, gratitude, and a commitment to live in accordance with God's will, reflecting the transformative power of Jesus' sacrifice in their lives. It reassures us that no matter how great our failings, God's love is greater still, offering hope and redemption to all who believe.

Redemption

Redemption involves being set free from the bondage of sin through the payment of a price, which Jesus paid with His blood. As Ephesians 1:7 states, "In Him we have redemption through His blood, the forgiveness of sins, in accordance with the riches of God's grace." This redemption restores the relationship between God and humanity that sin had broken, demonstrating that a transformed life must follow genuine faith.

Many people cherish the verse from John 3:16, which highlights God's immense love and the promise of eternal life through belief in His Son, Jesus Christ. "For God so loved the world, that he gave his only begotten Son, that whosoever believeth in him should not perish, but have everlasting life." This verse encapsulates the essence of the gospel and offers hope to disciples. However, it is equally important to remember Jesus' words in Matthew 7:21-23, where He cautions that mere verbal acknowledgment of His lordship is insufficient for entry into the kingdom of heaven: "Not every one that saith unto me, Lord, Lord, shall enter into the kingdom of heaven; but he that doeth the will of my Father which is in heaven."

This passage emphasizes that true faith must be accompanied by obedience to God's will, underscoring that belief alone is not enough.

Reconciliation

Reconciliation, on the other hand, is the restoration of the broken relationship between humanity and God. 2 Corinthians 5:18-19 explains, "All this is from God, who reconciled us to himself through Christ and gave us the ministry of reconciliation: that God was reconciling the world to himself in Christ, not counting people's sins against them." Through Christ's sacrifice, disciples are not only redeemed but also brought back into a harmonious relationship with God. This reconciliation is a profound aspect of salvation, highlighting that God's grace extends beyond forgiveness to the renewal of a personal relationship with Him. Thus, while John 3:16 offers the promise of eternal life through belief in Jesus, the call to live according to God's will, as emphasized in Matthew 7:21-23, and the transformative power of redemption and reconciliation must be embraced to fully experience the depth of God's salvation plan.

The Power of the Cross

The crucifixion is not just a past event but a present reality with ongoing implications for disciples. The cross stands as a symbol of victory over sin and death, offering hope and assurance of eternal life. Jesus' sacrifice on the cross was a pivotal moment in history, but its significance transcends time. For disciples today, the crucifixion remains a powerful reminder of God's love and the ultimate price paid for their redemption. It assures them that, despite the presence of sin and death in the world, victory has already been secured through Jesus' death and resurrection. This assurance gives disciples hope and strengthens their faith, knowing that eternal life is promised to them.

Through Jesus' sacrifice, disciples are called to live transformed lives, characterized by the same love and selflessness that He demonstrated. The power of the cross is not merely symbolic but transformative, calling disciples to embody the principles of sacrifice, humility, and love in their daily lives. This transformation is a response to the grace received through the crucifixion, leading disciples to live in a manner that reflects their gratitude and commitment to Christ. The crucifixion compels disciples to turn away from sinful behaviors and strive towards living a life that honors the sacrifice of Jesus, continually seeking to grow in holiness and righteousness.

The power of the cross enables disciples to overcome sin and live in the freedom and newness of life that Jesus secured through His death. Galatians 2:20 captures this transformative power: "I have been crucified with Christ and I no longer live, but Christ lives in me. The life I now live in the body, I live by faith in the Son of God, who loved me and gave himself for me." This verse highlights the profound change that occurs within a disciple who identifies with the crucifixion of Christ. It signifies that their old, sinful nature has been crucified, and they now live through the power of Christ within them. This new life is marked by faith, love, and a commitment to follow Jesus, empowered to resist sin and live in the freedom that His sacrifice has granted. Through the ongoing reality of the crucifixion, disciples are continually renewed and strengthened to live out their faith in a transformative way.

The Response to the Crucifixion

The appropriate response to the crucifixion is one of faith, gratitude, and obedience. Disciples are called to put their trust in Jesus, acknowledging His sacrifice as the means of their salvation. This faith is not merely intellectual assent but a profound trust in the redemptive work of Christ, recognizing that through His death and resurrection, they have been reconciled to God. By placing their faith in Jesus, disciples accept His gift of grace, understanding that it is not their works but His sacrifice that secures their salvation. This faith is foundational, leading disciples into a transformative relationship with God.

This faith naturally leads to a life of gratitude, where the enormity of Jesus' sacrifice compels disciples to live in a manner worthy of the gospel. Gratitude for the cross shapes every aspect of a disciple's life, influencing their thoughts, actions, and relationships. It becomes the driving force behind their desire to honor God in all they do. The realization of what Jesus endured on their behalf fosters a deep sense of thankfulness, motivating them to live selflessly and to serve others as an expression of their appreciation for His love. This gratitude is not passive but active, manifesting in a commitment to live out the principles of the gospel daily.

Obedience to God's commandments and a commitment to follow Jesus' example of love and selflessness become natural expressions of this gratitude. The crucifixion not only secures eternal life for disciples but also transforms their present lives, motivating them to live for God's glory. As disciples reflect on Jesus' sacrifice, they are inspired to emulate His humility, compassion, and obedience to the Father. This leads to a life marked by ethical integrity, sacrificial love, and a steadfast commitment to God's will. In living this way, disciples honor the crucifixion and demonstrate the transformative power of the gospel, bearing witness to the world of the hope and redemption found in Jesus Christ.

The Ultimate Sacrifice

The crucifixion of Jesus Christ is central to the gospel, encapsulating the gravity of sin and the extent of God's love. Through His sacrificial death, Jesus bore the penalty for humanity's sins, offering redemption and reconciliation with God. The power of the cross transforms disciples' lives, calling them to live in faith, gratitude, and obedience. This pivotal event in history continues to shape the lives of disciples, reminding them of the profound love of God and the hope of eternal life secured through Jesus' ultimate sacrifice.

Chapter 5: The Resurrection

The Prophecy

The resurrection of Jesus Christ stands as the cornerstone and focal point as a disciple, fulfilling numerous Old Testament prophecies and Jesus' own predictions. In the Psalms, David prophesied about the resurrection in Psalm 16:10, declaring, "For you will not abandon my soul to Sheol, or let your holy one see corruption." This verse is often interpreted as a prophecy of the Messiah's resurrection, affirming that God would not allow His chosen one to remain in the grave.

Moreover, Isaiah 53:10-11 speaks prophetically about the suffering and resurrection of the Messiah, stating, "Yet it was the will of the Lord to crush him; he has put him to grief; when his soul makes an offering for guilt, he shall see his offspring; he shall prolong his days; the will of the Lord shall prosper in his hand. Out of the anguish of his soul he shall see and be satisfied; by his knowledge shall the righteous one, my servant, make many to be accounted righteous, and he shall bear their iniquities." This passage foretells the Messiah's sacrificial death and subsequent resurrection, emphasizing the redemptive purpose of His suffering.

Jesus Himself prophesied His own death and resurrection, using the metaphor of the temple to explain His future resurrection. In John 2:19-21, Jesus said to the Hebrews, "Destroy this temple, and in three days I will raise it up." The Hebrews then said, "It has taken forty-six years to build this temple, and will you raise it up in three days?" But he was speaking about the temple of his body." This statement, along with similar predictions in Matthew 12:39-40 and Matthew 16:21, demonstrates Jesus' foreknowledge of His impending death and resurrection, indicating that His resurrection was not an unexpected event but a fulfillment of divine prophecy and purpose.

The resurrection of Jesus Christ is thus deeply rooted in both Old Testament prophecy and Jesus' own teachings, affirming His identity as the promised Messiah and the Son of God. This miraculous event not only validated Jesus' teachings and the truth of His message but also became the central testimony of early disciples, proclaiming that through His resurrection, Jesus conquered sin and death, offering eternal life to all who believe in Him.

First Fruits

In both the old and new covenant, the concept of first fruits holds profound spiritual significance, symbolizing dedication, gratitude, and the promise of abundant blessings. In the Old Covenant, the Feast of First Fruits was celebrated during the week of Unleavened Bread, marking the beginning of the barley harvest and offering the first portion of the harvest as an offering to God. Leviticus 23:10-11 outlines this practice: "Speak to the people of Israel and say to them, 'When you come into the land that I give you and reap its harvest, you shall bring the sheaf of the first fruits of your harvest to the priest, and he shall wave the sheaf before the Lord, so that you may be accepted. On the day after the Sabbath the priest shall wave it.'"

In the New Covenant, Jesus Christ's resurrection is likened to the first fruits offering in the Old Testament, signifying the beginning of a new spiritual harvest—the redemption and resurrection of disciples. 1 Corinthians 15:20-23 draws this parallel: "But in fact Christ has been raised from the dead, the firstfruits of those who have fallen asleep. For as by a man came death, by a man has come also the resurrection of the dead. For as in Adam all die, so also in Christ shall all be made alive. But each in his own order: Christ the firstfruits, then at his coming those who belong to Christ."

By identifying Jesus as the first fruits of those who have been raised from the dead, Paul emphasizes the significance of Christ's resurrection as the guarantee and precursor of the resurrection of all disciples. This pivotal event not only demonstrates Jesus' victory over death and sin but also inaugurates a new era where disciples share in His resurrection life. Just as the first fruits offering sanctified the harvest and acknowledged God's provision in the Old Testament, Christ's resurrection sanctifies and assures the hope of eternal life for all who are united with Him through faith. Therefore, the Feast of First Fruits is celebrated by disciples of Christ as a commemoration of Christ's resurrection, holding profound spiritual meaning, affirming the promise of new life and abundant blessings through the risen Savior.

Assurance of a Restored Relationship with God

For disciples, the resurrection of Jesus Christ is not merely a historical event but a profound demonstration of God's power and love, signifying the hope of eternal life and the assurance of a restored relationship with Him. The resurrection stands as the ultimate victory over sin and death, accomplished through Jesus' sacrificial death on the cross and His triumphant rising from the grave. Romans 4:25 states, "He was delivered over to death for our sins and was raised to life for our justification," underscoring that through His resurrection, Jesus secured forgiveness and reconciliation for all who place their faith in Him.

Through His resurrection, Jesus Christ offers disciples the assurance of a restored relationship with God, where the barrier of sin has been removed and communion with God is made possible. 2 Corinthians 5:18-19 affirms, "All this is from God, who reconciled us to himself through Christ and gave us the ministry of reconciliation: that God was reconciling the world to himself in Christ, not counting people's sins against them." This reconciliation is a central theme of the gospel, highlighting God's initiative in bridging the gap caused by sin and inviting humanity into a renewed relationship with Him.

The assurance of a restored relationship with God through the resurrection extends beyond forgiveness to encompass a transformed life empowered by the Holy Spirit. Ephesians 2:4-5 explains, "But because of his great love for us, God, who is rich in mercy, made us alive with Christ even when we were dead in transgressions—it is by grace you have been saved." Disciples are invited into a new life of fellowship with God, marked by intimacy, obedience, and the ongoing work of sanctification. Thus, the resurrection of Jesus Christ stands as the cornerstone of a disciple's faith, offering disciples the hope of eternal life and the assurance of a restored and vibrant relationship with God, grounded in His grace and redeeming love.

The New Era

Furthermore, the resurrection serves as a powerful demonstration of the transformative power of the gospel. It marks the beginning of a new era where disciples are invited to live in the reality of Christ's victory. As Romans 6:4 proclaims, "Therefore we were buried with Him through baptism into death, that just as Christ was raised from the dead by the glory of the Father, even so we also should walk in newness of life." This newness of life encompasses spiritual rebirth, a renewed purpose in serving God, and a commitment to living out the principles of the kingdom of God. The resurrection challenges disciples to embrace the full implications of their faith, recognizing that they are called to bear witness to the transformative power of Jesus' resurrection in their own lives and to share this hope with the world.

The resurrection of Jesus Christ not only confirms His victory over sin and death but also serves as the ultimate sign of God's love and grace toward humanity. It is through the resurrection that disciples find assurance that their sins are forgiven and that they have eternal life with God. This event reshapes their understanding of suffering, death, and hope, offering a profound sense of purpose and identity in Christ. Jesus' resurrection is central in the faith of Christ's disciples, symbolizing the promise of new beginnings and the triumph of light over darkness. As disciples reflect on the significance of the resurrection, they are invited to live with hope and courage, knowing that the same power that raised Jesus from the dead is at work in their lives. This chapter on the resurrection calls disciples to deepen their faith, embrace the transformative power of the gospel, and proclaim the hope of resurrection to a world in need of redemption and renewal.

Victory in the Resurrection

Christ's resurrection is the victory of the gospel because it signifies His triumph over sin and death, offering disciples the promise of eternal life. By rising from the dead on the third day, Jesus demonstrated His power over the grave, affirming His identity as the Son of God and validating His teachings. This victory over death is a cornerstone of a disciple's faith, as it provides the foundation for the hope of disciples. As the Apostle Paul states in 1 Corinthians 15:17, "And if Christ has not been raised, your faith is futile; you are still in your sins." The resurrection assures disciples that their faith is not in vain and that they, too, can look forward to their own resurrection and eternal life with God.

The resurrection also represents the fulfillment of God's redemptive plan for humanity. Throughout the Old Testament, prophecies hinted at a coming Messiah who would suffer, die, and rise again to redeem His people (Isaiah 53:10-12, Psalm 16:10). Jesus' resurrection fulfills these prophecies, confirming that He is the promised Savior. This act of divine intervention not only demonstrates God's faithfulness to His promises but also His immense love for humanity. By conquering death, Jesus opened the way for disciples to be reconciled with God, offering forgiveness for sins and restoring the broken relationship between God and humanity.

Furthermore, Christ's resurrection empowers disciples to live transformed lives. The power that raised Jesus from the dead is the same power that works in disciples, enabling them to overcome sin and live in newness of life. As Paul writes in Romans 6:4, "Therefore we were buried with Him through baptism into death, that just as Christ was raised from the dead by the glory of the Father, even so we also should walk in newness of life." This transformative power of the resurrection motivates disciples to follow Christ's example, embodying His love, compassion, and righteousness in their daily lives. Thus, the resurrection is not just a past event but a present reality that continually shapes and inspires the lives of those who follow Jesus.

Chapter 6: The Ascension

Significance of the Ascension

The ascension of Jesus Christ, as recorded in Acts 1:9-11, is a pivotal event in the faith of a disciple that signifies His exaltation and return to the Father. After His resurrection, Jesus appeared to His disciples and others over a period of forty days, teaching them about the kingdom of God and preparing them for the mission ahead. On the fortieth day, Jesus led His disciples to the Mount of Olives, where He gave them final instructions and blessed them. As they watched, He was taken up into heaven, and a cloud hid Him from their sight. This dramatic event marked the end of Jesus' earthly ministry and His return to His heavenly throne, where He now intercedes for disciples.

The ascension signifies the exaltation of Jesus and His return to the Father. Having completed His redemptive work on earth through His death and resurrection, Jesus ascended to His rightful place at the right hand of God. This position of honor and authority reflects His divine nature and the fulfillment of His mission. From this exalted position, Jesus continues to work on behalf of disciples, interceding for them and ensuring their ultimate salvation. The Apostle Paul emphasizes this in Ephesians 1:20-21, stating that God "raised Christ from the dead and seated him at his right hand in the heavenly realms, far above all rule and authority, power and dominion, and every name that is invoked, not only in the present age but also in the one to come."

The ascension also marks the beginning of the church's mission. Before His departure, Jesus gave His disciples the Great Commission, instructing them to "go and make disciples of all nations, baptizing them in the name of the Father and of the Son and of the Holy Spirit, and teaching them to obey everything I have commanded you" (Matthew 28:19-20). Jesus promised to send the Holy Spirit to empower His followers for this monumental task. The coming of the Holy Spirit on Pentecost, as recorded in Acts 2, fulfilled this promise and equipped the disciples to carry on Jesus' work, spreading the gospel and establishing the early church. Through the ascension, Jesus assured His followers of His ongoing presence and guidance, empowering them to fulfill their mission on earth.

Jesus' Authority

Jesus sitting at the right hand of His Father signifies His supreme authority and honor in the heavenly realm.

This position is one of power and prestige, indicating that Jesus has been exalted above all creation and now shares in the Father's glory and rule. The imagery of sitting at the right hand of God is drawn from ancient royal court practices, where the most trusted and powerful advisor to the king would sit at his right hand. In this exalted position, Jesus is recognized as the sovereign Lord who has triumphed over sin, death, and all opposing forces, fulfilling His redemptive work and establishing His eternal dominion.

This exaltation to the right hand of the Father also highlights Jesus' unique role as the mediator between God and humanity. As our High Priest, Jesus intercedes on behalf of disciples, presenting their prayers and needs before the Father. Hebrews 7:25 emphasizes this role, stating that Jesus "always lives to make intercession for them." This ongoing intercession ensures that disciples have a constant advocate in heaven, who understands their struggles and pleads their case. Jesus' presence at the right hand of the Father provides disciples with the assurance that they are not alone in their spiritual journey, as they have a powerful ally who continuously intercedes for them.

Furthermore, Jesus sitting at the right hand of the Father signifies the completion and fulfillment of His earthly mission. Having accomplished the work of salvation through His life, death, and resurrection, Jesus' ascension to this position marks the culmination of God's redemptive plan. Ephesians 1:20-21 describes this exaltation, noting that God raised Christ from the dead and seated Him at His right hand in the heavenly realms, far above all rule and authority, power and dominion. This exaltation not only validates Jesus' mission but also assures disciples of their future hope. As Jesus reigns in glory, He prepares a place for His followers, promising them a share in His eternal kingdom and the fullness of life in God's presence.

Jesus as Intercessory for Disciples

Jesus' intercessory role for disciples marks a significant shift from the Old Covenant to the New Covenant. Under the Old Covenant, intercession was conducted by priests who offered sacrifices and prayers on behalf of the people. These priests acted as mediators between God and humanity, continually offering sacrifices to atone for the sins of the people. However, these sacrifices were temporary and had to be repeated regularly. In contrast, Jesus, through His sacrificial death and resurrection, fulfilled and surpassed the Old Covenant's requirements. As the ultimate High Priest, Jesus' single sacrifice on the cross provides a permanent solution for sin, rendering the repeated sacrifices of the Old Covenant obsolete.

Jesus' intercessory role is not limited to a single act but is an ongoing ministry. Seated at the right hand of God, Jesus continuously advocates for His disciples, ensuring their needs and prayers are brought before the Father. This intercession is described in Hebrews 7:25, which states, "Therefore he is able to save completely those who come to God through him, because he always lives to intercede for them." Unlike the priests of the Old Covenant, who had to offer sacrifices repeatedly, Jesus' intercession is eternal and perfect, providing disciples with constant access to God's grace and mercy. His role as an intercessor highlights His deep love and commitment to His followers, ensuring their spiritual well-being and growth.

In the life of His disciples, Jesus' intercession is active and transformative. It ensures that disciples are continually supported and guided in their faith journey. Through His intercession, Jesus provides strength in times of weakness, comfort in times of sorrow, and guidance in times of confusion. This active involvement is a testament to His promise never to leave nor forsake His followers (Hebrews 13:5). Disciples can approach God with confidence, knowing that Jesus is interceding on their behalf. This ongoing intercession fosters a profound sense of intimacy and assurance, empowering disciples to live out their faith with boldness and conviction. Jesus' intercessory role under the New Covenant thus represents a dynamic and enduring relationship between Him and His disciples, marked by His constant presence and unwavering support.

The Beginning of the Church's Mission

The ascension also marks the beginning of the church's mission. Before His departure, Jesus gave His disciples the Great Commission, instructing them to "go and make disciples of all nations, baptizing them in the name of the Father and of the Son and of the Holy Spirit, and teaching them to obey everything I have commanded you" (Matthew 28:19-20). Jesus promised to send the Holy Spirit to empower His followers for this monumental task. In Acts 1:8, He told them, "But you will receive power when the Holy Spirit comes on you; and you will be my witnesses in Jerusalem, and in all Judea and Samaria, and to the ends of the earth." The coming of the Holy Spirit on Pentecost, as recorded in Acts 2, fulfilled this promise and equipped the disciples to carry on Jesus' work, spreading the gospel and establishing the early church.

Chapter 7: The Holy Spirit

The outpouring of the Holy Spirit, which is the spirit of God, is a profound and significant aspect of the gospel. While the Holy Spirit has always been around, Jesus promised His disciples that the Holy Spirit would be sent to guide, comfort, and empower them after his ascension. This promise was fulfilled on the day of Pentecost, marking the beginning of the Spirit's transformative work in the lives of disciples. The Holy Spirit enables disciples to live according to God's will and to be witnesses of the gospel to the ends of the earth.

The Promise of the Holy Spirit

Jesus spoke extensively about the coming of the Holy Spirit. In the Gospel of John, He reassures His disciples of this promise, saying, "And I will pray the Father, and he shall give you another Comforter, that he may abide with you for ever; Even the Spirit of truth; whom the world cannot receive, because it seeth him not, neither knoweth him: but ye know him; for he dwelleth with you, and shall be in you" (John 14:16-17). This promise underscores the role of the Holy Spirit as a permanent presence in the lives of disciples, offering guidance and truth.

Further, in John 16:7-13, Jesus explains the necessity and benefits of the Holy Spirit's coming: "Nevertheless I tell you the truth; It is expedient for you that I go away: for if I go not away, the Comforter will not come unto you; but if I depart, I will send him unto you. And when he is come, he will reprove the world of sin, and of righteousness, and of judgment: Of sin, because they believe not on me; Of righteousness, because I go to my Father, and ye see me no more; Of judgment, because the prince of this world is judged. I have yet many things to say unto you, but ye cannot bear them now. Howbeit when he, the Spirit of truth, is come, he will guide you into all truth: for he shall not speak of himself; but whatsoever he shall hear, that shall he speak: and he will shew you things to come."

The Fulfillment at Pentecost

The fulfillment of Jesus' promise is vividly depicted in the book of Acts. On the day of Pentecost, the disciples were gathered in one place when the Holy Spirit descended upon them. Acts 2:1-4 records this momentous event: "And when the day of Pentecost was fully come, they were all with one accord in one place. And suddenly there came a sound from heaven as of a rushing mighty wind, and it filled all the house where they were sitting. And there appeared unto them cloven tongues like as of fire, and it sat upon each of them. And they were all filled with the Holy Ghost, and began to speak with other tongues, as the Spirit gave them utterance."

This outpouring of the Holy Spirit empowered the disciples in unprecedented ways. They began to speak in different languages, enabling them to communicate the gospel to people from various nations who had gathered in Jerusalem. This miraculous sign not only validated their message but also demonstrated the inclusivity of the gospel, breaking down linguistic and cultural barriers.

The Role of the Holy Spirit in the Disciple's Life

The Holy Spirit plays a crucial role in the life of every disciple. He is the source of spiritual regeneration and renewal. As Jesus explained to Nicodemus, "Except a man be born of water and of the Spirit, he cannot enter into the kingdom of God" (John 3:5). The Spirit's work in regeneration is essential for salvation, transforming the disciple's heart and mind.

Additionally, the Holy Spirit serves as a guide and teacher. John 14:26 states, "But the Comforter, which is the Holy Ghost, whom the Father will send in my name, he shall teach you all things, and bring all things to your remembrance, whatsoever I have said unto you." This divine instruction helps disciples understand and apply the truths of Scripture, leading them into deeper spiritual maturity.

Empowerment for Witness

One of the primary functions of the Holy Spirit is to empower disciples to be witnesses of the gospel. Jesus emphasized this in Acts 1:8, saying, "But ye shall receive power, after that the Holy Spirit is come upon you: and ye shall be witnesses unto me both in Jerusalem, and in all Judaea, and in Samaria, and unto the uttermost part of the earth." This empowerment is essential for fulfilling the Great Commission, enabling disciples to proclaim the gospel boldly and effectively.

The Apostle Paul experienced this empowerment firsthand and described its impact in his ministry. In 1 Corinthians 2:4-5, he writes, "And my speech and my preaching was not with enticing words of man's wisdom, but in demonstration of the Spirit and of power: That your faith should not stand in the wisdom of men, but in the power of God." The Holy Spirit's power transforms ordinary disciples into powerful witnesses, capable of performing miracles, proclaiming truth, and living lives that reflect Christ's love and righteousness.

The Holy Spirit's Continued Presence

The presence of the Holy Spirit is a continual source of comfort and strength for disciples. Romans 8:26-27 highlights the Spirit's role in prayer: "Likewise the Spirit also helpeth our infirmities: for we know not what we should pray for as we ought: but the Spirit itself maketh intercession for us with groanings which cannot be uttered. And he that searcheth the hearts knoweth what is the mind of the Spirit, because he maketh intercession for the saints according to the will of God." This intercessory work ensures that disciples are always aligned with God's will, even in their prayers.

Fruits of the Spirit

The Holy Spirit produces spiritual fruit in the lives of disciples, as described in Galatians 5:22-23: "But the fruit of the Spirit is love, joy, peace, longsuffering, gentleness, goodness, faith, Meekness, temperance: against such there is no law." These nine attributes collectively represent the visible evidence of the Spirit's transformative power within a person's life. Each of these fruits highlights a specific aspect of the character and behavior that should be evident in someone who is living under the influence of the Holy Spirit.

Love, the first mentioned fruit, epitomizes the selfless, unconditional care that reflects God's love for humanity. This love is not based on emotions or conditions but is a deliberate choice to seek the best for others, mirroring the sacrificial love of Christ. Joy and peace follow, embodying a deep-seated, unwavering sense of contentment and tranquility that persist regardless of external circumstances. Joy comes from an internal assurance in God's sovereignty, while peace is a calmness that stems from trusting in His control over all situations.

Longsuffering, or patience, is another crucial fruit, enabling disciples to endure challenges and setbacks with a calm and forgiving heart. This patience allows for the bearing of others' faults and the willingness to wait for God's timing. It often goes hand in hand with gentleness, a characteristic marked by kindness and a compassionate demeanor toward others. These traits help disciples to respond to others with empathy and understanding, fostering stronger, more harmonious relationships. Gentleness is about showing care and respect, especially in how we treat those around us.

Goodness signifies a moral integrity and a desire to act virtuously, reflecting God's righteousness in everyday actions. It is about doing what is right and just, even when it is difficult. This attribute drives disciples to seek and uphold truth, demonstrating God's character in practical ways. Faith, or faithfulness, underscores reliability and steadfastness in one's relationship with God and others. It implies a deep trust in God's promises and a commitment to live out His will, showing loyalty and dependability.

Meekness, often misunderstood as weakness, actually represents strength under control, a humility that acknowledges God's sovereignty and one's own need for His guidance. This humility enables disciples to approach life and others with a sense of grace and restraint, avoiding arrogance and pride. Meekness involves putting others before oneself and maintaining a gentle attitude, even in the face of provocation.

Temperance, or self-control, is the final fruit mentioned and is essential for maintaining a balanced, disciplined life. This attribute empowers disciples to resist temptations and make choices that honor God, reflecting an inner strength and resolve. Self-control is about governing one's desires and actions, ensuring that they align with God's standards. Collectively, these characteristics are not just abstract ideals but practical, visible expressions of a life transformed by the Holy Spirit. They enable disciples to live out their faith in tangible ways, demonstrating the profound impact of God's presence in their lives.

Conclusion

The gift of the Holy Spirit is an essential aspect of a disciples faith, fulfilling Jesus' promise to His followers. From the dramatic events of Pentecost to the ongoing work of regeneration, guidance, empowerment, and intercession, the Holy Spirit plays a crucial role in the life of every disciple. Through the Spirit, disciples are equipped to live according to God's will, proclaim the gospel boldly, and experience the fullness of their relationship with God. The presence of the Holy Spirit is a continual reminder of God's love and power, guiding and sustaining disciples as they fulfill their mission on earth.

Chapter 8: The Church

The Commonwealth of Israel

The Church, in its truest sense, is the commonwealth of Israel, a unified spiritual nation encompassing both Israelites and Gentiles grafted in through faith in Jesus Christ. In modern times, many people perceive the church primarily as a physical building, a denomination, or a specific congregation. However, the biblical understanding of the church transcends these limited views. The church is a collective body of disciples, a spiritual nation bound together by their faith in Christ, forming a commonwealth that bridges the historical divide between Israel and the Gentiles.

A commonwealth is defined as a political community founded for the common good. This concept beautifully aligns with the church's mission, as it is a community of disciples working together for the common good under the lordship of Christ. Before Christ's ascension, God's dealings were primarily focused on His chosen nation, Israel. Jesus instructed His disciples to go to the lost sheep of the house of Israel, emphasizing the priority of the Israelite people in God's redemptive plan (Matthew 10:5-6). However, after His resurrection, Jesus expanded this mission, instructing His disciples to go and make disciples of all nations (Matthew 28:19), thus opening the door for Gentiles to become part of the spiritual commonwealth.

The Apostle Paul played a pivotal role in spreading this mission and clarifying the nature of the church. Paul's teachings emphasized that in Christ, there is neither Jew nor Gentile, but all are one (Galatians 3:28). This radical inclusivity underscored the church as a unified body of disciples, regardless of ethnic or cultural backgrounds. The early church operated with this unity, working together as one strong, cohesive force for the gospel's advancement. Paul himself embodied this mission, traveling extensively to preach to both Jews and Gentiles, establishing communities of disciples that reflected this new commonwealth.

In contrast, the modern church is often segmented and divided, differing significantly from the foundations laid by the early church. Denominationalism, doctrinal disputes, and cultural differences have led to a fractured body, far removed from the original vision of unity. Yet, all disciples of Christ are the church, a truth that remains constant regardless of these divisions. The early church's model serves as a reminder and a challenge for contemporary disciples to strive for greater unity and cooperation, focusing on the common good and the shared mission of spreading the gospel.

We Don't Go to Church, We Are the Church

Today, many people speak of "going to church," not recognizing that the church is not a place one attends but a community one belongs to. This common misconception reduces the church to mere buildings and weekly gatherings, overlooking its true essence as a living, dynamic body of disciples. The church is fundamentally about the people who comprise it, united in their faith in Jesus Christ. This collective identity should inform and inspire their actions, leading to a deeper understanding of what it means to be part of the church. Recognizing that disciples themselves are the church shifts the focus from physical structures to the relationships and shared mission that bind them together.

Being part of the church means actively participating in the mission of Christ, contributing to the commonwealth of disciples, and working together to fulfill God's purposes on earth. This involves more than attending services; it requires engagement, service, and collaboration within the community. Every disciple has a role to play in advancing the gospel, supporting one another, and addressing the needs of the broader society. By embracing their identity as the church, disciples are called to live out their faith in practical, impactful ways, embodying the love, compassion, and justice that Christ exemplified.

This perspective shifts the focus from physical locations and institutional structures to the relational and communal aspects of the faith. The early church thrived on the strength of its community, characterized by shared meals, communal prayer, and mutual support. Modern disciples can learn from this model by prioritizing relationships, fostering genuine connections, and working together towards common goals. Understanding the church as a community of disciples encourages a more holistic and engaged approach to faith, where the emphasis is on living out the teachings of Christ in everyday life, supporting one another, and collectively pursuing God's mission in the world.

The Works

Another vital aspect of the church's mission is to serve as the hands and feet of Jesus in the world, embodying His love and compassion through acts of service and justice. This means going beyond the walls of the church building to address the needs of the broader community and world. The church is called to minister to the physical, emotional, and spiritual needs of individuals and communities, following Jesus' example of healing the sick, feeding the hungry, and caring for the marginalized. By actively engaging in these acts of service, the church not only meets immediate needs but also demonstrates the transformative power of the gospel.

This mission of service is an essential expression of the gospel, demonstrating God's love in tangible ways and working towards the restoration and reconciliation of all creation. Jesus' ministry was marked by acts of compassion and justice, and the church is called to continue this work. Through its various ministries and outreach programs, the church seeks to transform lives and communities, reflecting the kingdom of God on earth. Whether it is through food banks, medical missions, educational initiatives, or social justice advocacy, the church's mission is to be a beacon of hope and a force for good in the world.

The church should operate as a nation, utilizing the vocations wherewith we are called to help one another. The concept of the church as the Commonwealth of Israel highlights the importance of interdependence and mutual support among disciples. By fostering a self-sufficient community, the church can more effectively meet the needs of its members and extend its reach to those outside the faith. This self-sufficiency does not imply isolation but rather a robust internal support system that allows the church to operate independently of external pressures and influences. When the church relies on its own resources and the gifts of its members, it is better positioned to fulfill its mission and witness to the world.

The ultimate goal is for the Commonwealth of Israel, the church, to become fully self-sufficient, gaining its truest power. Self-sufficiency in the church means not needing anything from the world that could compromise its mission or values. It means having the resources, both material and spiritual, to carry out its work without relying on external support that may come with strings attached. When the church becomes self-sufficient, it can focus entirely on its mission to serve, transform, and restore. It can fully embody the love and compassion of Jesus, operate with integrity and independence, and demonstrate the power of the gospel to change lives and communities. This self-sufficiency empowers the church to be a true reflection of the kingdom of God, standing as a testament to His provision and faithfulness.

Fellowship

Fellowship is a vital component of the church's mission, fostering a community of disciples who worship, grow, and support one another in their faith journeys. The church provides a sacred space for corporate worship, where disciples come together to glorify God, receive teaching and encouragement, and partake in the sacraments. This collective worship experience not only honors God but also reinforces the bonds among disciples, creating a sense of unity and shared purpose. Regular gatherings for worship, including services, prayer meetings, and celebrations of the Lord's Supper, help to maintain a strong communal identity rooted in faith and devotion.

Additionally, the church offers numerous opportunities for spiritual growth through Bible studies, prayer groups, and discipleship programs. These activities are designed to deepen disciples' understanding of Scripture, strengthen their prayer lives, and cultivate their personal relationship with God. By engaging in these spiritual disciplines together, members of the church can encourage and challenge one another, fostering an environment where faith can flourish. Discipleship programs, in particular, provide mentorship and guidance, helping individuals to mature in their faith and develop the skills needed to live out their beliefs in practical, everyday ways.

By nurturing a sense of fellowship and unity, the church strengthens the faith of its members, equipping them to engage in the broader mission of evangelism and service. This communal aspect of the church's mission ensures that disciples are supported, challenged, and empowered to fulfill their calling as followers of Christ. Through mutual support and shared experiences, members of the church are better prepared to face life's challenges, maintain their faith, and extend God's love to others. In this way, the church not only fosters individual spiritual growth but also builds a strong, cohesive community dedicated to living out the gospel and impacting the world for Christ.

Chapter 9: The High Holy Days

The biblical calendar is marked by seven high holy days, along with the Sabbath and the observance of new moons, which hold profound significance in the life of Disciples of Christ. These sacred times were instituted by God to provide His people with opportunities for worship, reflection, and renewal. Understanding these holy days helps disciples appreciate the rhythm of God's redemptive work throughout history and its fulfillment in Jesus Christ.

1. The Sabbath

The Sabbath is the weekly day of rest and worship, observed from Friday evening to Saturday evening. It commemorates God's rest after creating the world (Genesis 2:2-3) and serves as a sign of the covenant between God and His people (Exodus 31:13-17). The Sabbath is a time to cease from labor, reflect on God's creation, and enjoy rest. It foreshadows the ultimate rest found in Jesus, who offers rest for our souls (Matthew 11:28-30). For disciples, the principle of the Sabbath remains relevant as a reminder to set aside time for rest, worship, and renewal.

2. New Moons

The observance of new moons marks the beginning of each month in the Hebrew calendar. These monthly celebrations were times of special offerings and worship (Numbers 10:10, 28:11-15). They served as reminders of God's provision and sovereignty over time. The new moon festivals encouraged the community to pause and acknowledge God's faithfulness, aligning their lives with His divine order. Under the New Covenant, the concept of regularly acknowledging God's timing and provision remains significant.

3. Passover (Pesach)

Passover, celebrated in the first month of the biblical calendar (Nisan), commemorates the Israelites' deliverance from Egyptian slavery (Exodus 12). It involves the eating of a special meal, including lamb, unleavened bread, and bitter herbs. Passover prefigures Jesus Christ, the Lamb of God, whose sacrifice delivers disciples from the bondage of sin. The Last Supper, which Jesus shared with His disciples, was a Passover meal, linking His death to the liberation themes of Passover (1 Corinthians 5:7).

4. Feast of Unleavened Bread

Following Passover is the seven-day Feast of Unleavened Bread (Nisan 15-21), during which no leaven is eaten (Exodus 12:15-20). This festival commemorates the haste with which the Israelites left Egypt, without time for their bread to rise. Spiritually, it signifies the removal of sin (leaven) from one's life. For disciples, it symbolizes living a life of sincerity and truth, free from the corrupting influence of sin (1 Corinthians 5:8). It is celebrated with communion with unleavened bread representing the body of Christ and wine or grapejuice as the blood of Jesus.

5. Feast of Firstfruits

The Feast of Firstfruits occurs on the day after the Sabbath following Passover (Leviticus 23:9-14). It involves offering the first sheaf of the barley harvest to God, acknowledging His provision. This feast is significant for disciples as it celebrates Jesus' resurrection, the firstfruits of those who have fallen asleep (1 Corinthians 15:20). It celebrates the promise of new life and the future resurrection of disciples.

6. Feast of Weeks (Shavuot or Pentecost)

The Feast of Weeks, or Shavuot, is celebrated fifty days after Firstfruits (Leviticus 23:15-21). It marks the end of the grain harvest and commemorates the giving of the

Torah at Mount Sinai. For disciples, Pentecost (Acts 2) is the fulfillment of this feast, when the Holy Spirit was poured out on the disciples, empowering them to spread the gospel. It signifies the birth of the church and the new covenant written on disciples' hearts.

7. Feast of Trumpets (Rosh Hashanah)

The Feast of Trumpets, or Rosh Hashanah, marks the beginning of the seventh month (Tishri) (Leviticus 23:23-25). It is a time of blowing trumpets, signifying a call to repentance and a reminder of God's sovereignty. For disciples, it points to the future return of Christ, heralded by the sound of a trumpet (1 Thessalonians 4:16). It is a time to reflect on God's kingship and prepare for His coming judgment.

8. Day of Atonement (Yom Kippur)

The Day of Atonement, or Yom Kippur, is the holiest day of the biblical calendar (Leviticus 16, 23:26-32). It is a solemn day of fasting, prayer, and repentance, when the high priest would enter the Holy of Holies to make atonement for the sins of Israel. For disciples, Jesus' sacrifice on the cross is the ultimate fulfillment of Yom Kippur, providing eternal atonement for sin (Hebrews 9:11-12). It is a day to reflect on the seriousness of sin and the profound mercy of God.

9. Feast of Tabernacles (Sukkot)

The Feast of Tabernacles, or Sukkot, begins on the fifteenth day of the seventh month (Tishri) and lasts for seven days (Leviticus 23:33-43). It commemorates the Israelites' forty years of wandering in the wilderness, living in temporary shelters. It is a joyful festival celebrating God's provision and presence. For disciples, it looks forward to the ultimate fulfillment in the coming kingdom of God, where disciples will dwell with Him eternally (Revelation 21:3).

Conclusion

The seven high holy days, along with the Sabbath and new moons, are rich with significance and spiritual lessons. They provide a framework for understanding God's redemptive plan and His relationship with His people. These holy times invite disciples to reflect on their faith, recognize God's ongoing work in history, and live in anticipation of His promises. By observing and studying these biblical festivals, disciples can gain deeper insights into their faith and the continuity of God's salvation story from the Old Testament to the New Testament.

Chapter 10: The Dietary Laws

The dietary laws outlined in the Bible form a significant aspect of the Old Testament's guidance for holy living. These laws, found primarily in Leviticus 11 and Deuteronomy 14, distinguish between clean and unclean animals, providing God's people with specific instructions on what they can and cannot eat. While many Christians today believe that these dietary restrictions no longer apply under the New Covenant, a deeper understanding of these laws and their continued significance can offer valuable insights into living a life set apart for God.

Clean and Unclean Animals

The Bible's dietary laws are explicit about which animals are considered clean and fit for consumption, and which are unclean and should be avoided. These laws are primarily detailed in Leviticus 11 and Deuteronomy 14.

Clean Animals

1. **Land Animals**: Animals that have a split hoof completely divided and chew the cud are considered clean.

   o Examples: Cows, sheep, goats, and deer.

   o Bible Reference: Leviticus 11:3 - "Whatsoever parteth the hoof, and is clovenfooted, and cheweth the cud, among the beasts, that shall ye eat."

2. **Seafood**: Only fish with fins and scales are clean.

   o Examples: Salmon, trout, and cod.

   o Bible Reference: Leviticus 11:9 - "These shall ye eat of all that are in the waters: whatsoever hath fins and scales in the waters, in the seas, and in the rivers, them shall ye eat."

3. **Birds**: Certain birds are clean, though the Bible does not give a specific distinguishing feature for clean birds, it lists the unclean ones.

   o Examples: Chicken, turkey, and dove (clean by tradition and common understanding).

- Bible Reference: Deuteronomy 14:11 - "Of all clean birds ye shall eat."

4. **Insects**: Some insects are clean, specifically those that have jointed legs for hopping on the ground.

     - Examples: Locusts, crickets, and grasshoppers.

     - Bible Reference: Leviticus 11:22 - "Even these of them ye may eat; the locust after his kind, and the bald locust after his kind, and the beetle after his kind, and the grasshopper after his kind."

Unclean Animals

1. **Land Animals**: Animals that do not have both a split hoof and chew the cud are unclean.

     - Examples: Pigs, rabbits, and camels.

     - Bible Reference: Leviticus 11:7-8 - "And the swine, though he divide the hoof, and be clovenfooted, yet he cheweth not the cud; he is unclean to you. Of their flesh shall ye not eat, and their carcass shall ye not touch; they are unclean to you."

2. **Seafood**: Any sea creatures without fins and scales are unclean.

- Examples: Shrimp, crabs, lobsters, and catfish.

- Bible Reference: Leviticus 11:10 - "And all that have not fins and scales in the seas, and in the rivers, of all that move in the waters, and of any living thing which is in the waters, they shall be an abomination unto you."

3. **Birds**: Certain birds are specifically listed as unclean.

- Examples: Eagles, vultures, and owls.

- Bible Reference: Leviticus 11:13-19 - "And these are they which ye shall have in abomination among the fowls; they shall not be eaten, they are an abomination: the eagle, and the ossifrage, and the ospray, And the vulture, and the kite after his kind; Every raven after his kind; And the owl, and the night hawk, and the cuckow, and the hawk after his kind, And the little owl, and the cormorant, and the great owl, And the swan, and the pelican, and the gier eagle, And the stork, the heron after her kind, and the lapwing, and the bat."

4. **Insects**: Most insects are unclean, with exceptions only for certain locusts and similar creatures.

   ○ Bible Reference: Leviticus 11:20-23 - "All fowls that creep, going upon all four, shall be an abomination unto you."

Christians and Dietary Laws Today

Many Christians today do not observe the biblical dietary laws, often citing New Testament passages such as Acts 10:9-16, where Peter has a vision of a sheet with various animals and is told to kill and eat, signifying that what God has made clean should not be called impure. Additionally, Jesus' teaching in Mark 7:18-19 is interpreted by many as declaring all foods clean: "And he saith unto them, Are ye so without understanding also? Do ye not perceive, that whatsoever thing from without entereth into the man, it cannot defile him; Because it entereth not into his heart, but into the belly, and goeth out into the draught, purging all meats?"

However, it is essential to consider the broader context of these passages and the early church's discussions regarding Gentile converts and Israelite customs. While the New Testament does indicate a shift towards a new understanding of purity and defilement, rooted in the heart's condition rather than purely diet, the dietary laws' original intent and significance should not be dismissed. These laws were given to Israel as a means of setting them apart as a holy nation, reflecting God's desire for His people to live distinctively.

Significance and Application

The dietary laws are a means of maintaining a physical reminder of their spiritual commitment and identity. It is also be seen as a way to honor God's instructions and recognize the holistic nature of His concern for His people, encompassing not only spiritual but also physical aspects of life. Additionally, these laws can serve as a conversation starter, providing opportunities to share about faith and the principles behind these practices.

The underlying principles of holiness, obedience, and distinctiveness remain relevant. Disciples are called to live lives that reflect God's character and to be mindful of their actions, including their dietary choices, as expressions of their faith. Understanding and respecting these biblical dietary laws enhance one's appreciation of the continuity of God's revelation and the ways in which He calls His people to live set-apart lives.

Conclusion

In conclusion, the dietary laws of the Bible provide important insights into God's expectations for His people and the principles of holiness and obedience. While many Christians today do not adhere to these laws, recognizing their significance and the broader context within which they were given can enrich one's faith journey and understanding of biblical teachings. The call to live a life that honors God in all aspects remains central to the disciples of Christ.

Chapter 11: The Armor of God

The concept of the "full armor of God" is one of the most powerful and vivid metaphors used in the New Testament to describe the spiritual resources available to disciples. Found in Ephesians 6:10-18, this passage outlines a divine strategy for standing firm against the spiritual forces of evil. Each piece of armor represents a different aspect of spiritual readiness and defense, and understanding these elements is crucial for living a victorious Christ centered life.

The Belt of Truth

"Stand therefore, having your loins girt about with truth" (Ephesians 6:14). The belt of truth represents the disciple's integrity and commitment to God's truth. In a world filled with deception and relativism, truth serves as the foundation for a disciple's spiritual defense. Jesus declared, "I am the way, the truth, and the life" (John 14:6), emphasizing that truth is not just an abstract concept but personified in Christ Himself. Knowing and living by the truth of God's Word is essential for maintaining spiritual stability and discernment.

The Breastplate of Righteousness

"Having on the breastplate of righteousness" (Ephesians 6:14). The breastplate of righteousness protects the heart, symbolizing the righteousness that comes from God through faith in Jesus Christ. This righteousness is not our own but is imputed to us by God. As Paul writes in Philippians 3:9, "And be found in him, not having mine own righteousness, which is of the law, but that which is through the faith of Christ, the righteousness which is of God by faith." Living a righteous life guards the disciple's heart against the attacks of the enemy, ensuring moral integrity and uprightness.

The Shoes of the Gospel of Peace

"And your feet shod with the preparation of the gospel of peace" (Ephesians 6:15). The shoes of the gospel of peace enable disciples to stand firm and move forward, spreading the message of peace and reconciliation found in the gospel. Isaiah 52:7 proclaims, "How beautiful upon the mountains are the feet of him that bringeth good tidings, that publisheth peace; that bringeth good tidings of good, that publisheth salvation." Being prepared to share the gospel not only advances God's kingdom but also brings peace and stability to the disciple's own life.

The Shield of Faith

"Above all, taking the shield of faith, wherewith ye shall be able to quench all the fiery darts of the wicked" (Ephesians 6:16). The shield of faith represents a disciple's trust in God's promises and power. Faith acts as a defensive barrier against the attacks and temptations of the enemy. Hebrews 11:1 defines faith as "the substance of things hoped for, the evidence of things not seen." By holding firmly to faith, disciples can extinguish the doubts, fears, and lies that Satan uses to undermine their confidence in God.

The Helmet of Salvation

"And take the helmet of salvation" (Ephesians 6:17). The helmet of salvation protects the mind, symbolizing the assurance of salvation and the renewal of the mind through Christ. Romans 12:2 urges disciples, "And be not conformed to this world: but be ye transformed by the renewing of your mind." The knowledge and assurance of salvation provide a firm foundation for mental and emotional security, enabling disciples to withstand the enemy's attempts to shake their confidence in God's saving grace.

The Sword of the Spirit

"And the sword of the Spirit, which is the word of God" (Ephesians 6:17). The sword of the Spirit is the only offensive weapon in the armor of God, representing the power and authority of God's Word. Hebrews 4:12 describes the Word of God as "quick, and powerful, and sharper than any twoedged sword." Jesus Himself used Scripture to counter Satan's temptations in the wilderness (Matthew 4:1-11). Knowing and applying God's Word is crucial for both defense and advancing in spiritual battles.

Prayer: The Overarching Element

While not depicted as a piece of armor, prayer is essential in the spiritual battle. Ephesians 6:18 instructs, "Praying always with all prayer and supplication in the Spirit, and watching thereunto with all perseverance and supplication for all saints". Prayer energizes and activates the armor, ensuring that disciples remain connected to God, vigilant, and empowered. Philippians 4:6-7 reinforces the importance of prayer: "Be careful for nothing; but in every thing by prayer and supplication with thanksgiving let your requests be made known unto God. And the peace of God, which passeth all understanding, shall keep your hearts and minds through Christ Jesus."

The Significance of the Full Armor

The full armor of God is not merely a set of defensive measures but a comprehensive strategy for living a victorious Christ centered life. Each piece of armor reflects a vital aspect of a disciple's spiritual resources and responsibilities. By putting on the full armor, disciples can stand firm against the enemy's schemes, advance the gospel, and live lives that reflect the character and power of Christ.

Understanding and utilizing the full armor of God involves a daily commitment to truth, righteousness, the gospel, faith, salvation, and God's Word, all undergirded by constant prayer. This holistic approach to spiritual readiness enables disciples to navigate the challenges of life with confidence and resilience, knowing that they are fully equipped by God to overcome every obstacle and opposition.

The full armor of God provides a powerful framework for spiritual defense and growth. By embracing each element of the armor and integrating it into their daily lives, disciples can experience the fullness of God's protection, guidance, and strength, living victoriously in their faith and witness to the world.

Chapter 12: God's Laws

The Nature and Purpose of God's Laws

God's laws, as given in the Bible, serve multiple vital purposes that extend beyond mere legalistic requirements. Firstly, they reveal God's character, showcasing His holiness, justice, and love. By understanding and adhering to these laws, disciples can gain insight into the nature of God and His divine attributes. For instance, the Ten Commandments highlight God's moral perfection and His desire for a righteous relationship with His creation. As the psalmist expresses in Psalm 19:7, "The law of the Lord is perfect, converting the soul: the testimony of the Lord is sure, making wise the simple." This verse emphasizes that God's laws are flawless and transformative, guiding individuals toward spiritual enlightenment and wisdom.

Secondly, God's laws set moral standards that delineate right from wrong, providing a moral compass for disciples. These standards are not arbitrary but rooted in the intrinsic nature of God, reflecting His righteousness. The moral laws, such as those found in the Ten Commandments, address fundamental ethical principles like honesty, integrity, and respect for life and property. These commandments serve as timeless benchmarks for moral conduct, applicable to all generations. By adhering to these standards, disciples can lead lives that are pleasing to God, promote justice, and foster harmonious relationships within their communities.

Thirdly, God's laws guide social behavior and facilitate spiritual relationships between God and His people. The ceremonial and civil laws given in the Old Testament, while specific to the cultural and historical context of ancient Israel, illustrate how God's people are to conduct themselves in worship and daily life. These laws encompass various aspects of life, including dietary regulations, religious rituals, and social justice principles. Although the ceremonial laws were fulfilled in Christ, their underlying principles remain relevant, teaching disciples about holiness, reverence, and communal responsibility. Moreover, by following God's laws, disciples can cultivate a deeper spiritual connection with Him, recognizing their dependence on His grace and striving to live in accordance with His will. This comprehensive framework provided by God's laws ensures that disciples can honor God in all aspects of their lives, fostering a closer, more intimate relationship with their Creator.

Laws such as those forbidding incest and homosexuality serve to protect individuals and communities from the deceptions and moral relativism of the modern world. By upholding these standards, disciples are safeguarded against practices that can lead to physical, emotional, and spiritual harm. These laws are rooted in God's design for human relationships, promoting healthy and respectful interactions that honor the sanctity of family and sexual integrity. In a society where values are increasingly subjective, adhering to these divine commandments provides a clear and unchanging moral framework that resists the pressures of cultural shifts and societal trends. By following these laws, disciples maintain a commitment to God's truth, thereby avoiding the confusion and chaos that often accompany the rejection of biblical principles.

The Moral Law

The moral law, encapsulated in the Ten Commandments, forms the core ethical principles that govern human behavior. Found in Exodus 20:1-17 and reiterated in Deuteronomy 5:6-21, these commandments include:

1. **No other gods before Me:** (Exodus 20:3) God demands exclusive worship.

2. **No idols**: (Exodus 20:4-6) Worship should be directed to God alone, not to images.

3. **Do not take the Lord's name in vain**: (Exodus 20:7) God's name is to be honored.

4. **Remember the Sabbath day**: (Exodus 20:8-11) A day of rest and worship.

5. **Honor your father and mother**: (Exodus 20:12) Respect for parental authority.

6. **Do not murder**: (Exodus 20:13) Respect for human life.

7. **Do not commit adultery**: (Exodus 20:14) Faithfulness in marriage.

8. **Do not steal**: (Exodus 20:15) Respect for others' property.

9. **Do not bear false witness**: (Exodus 20:16) Truthfulness.

10. **Do not covet**: (Exodus 20:17) Contentment with what one has.

These laws are foundational and timeless, reflecting God's holy nature and providing a moral compass for humanity.

The Ceremonial Law

The ceremonial laws pertain to a disciple's worship practices, rituals, and festivals. These include laws about various festivals, such as Passover and the Day of Atonement (See Chapter 9). Found primarily in Leviticus, these laws are designed to set the Commonwealth of Israel (Christ's Disciples) apart as a holy nation and to foreshadow the coming of Christ. For example, Leviticus 16 describes the Day of Atonement, a significant ceremonial law highlighting the need for atonement and pointing to Christ's ultimate sacrifice.

The Civil Law

The civil laws are to govern the daily life and social interactions of disciples. These laws cover various aspects of community life, including property rights, justice, and interpersonal relationships. Examples of civil laws can be found in Exodus 21-23, which include regulations about restitution, treatment of servants, and legal justice. These laws ensure social order and reflect God's justice and compassion in societal dealings.

Dietary Laws

The dietary laws, found in Leviticus 11 and Deuteronomy 14, distinguish between clean and unclean foods (See Chapter 10). For instance, Leviticus

11:2-3 states, "These are the beasts which ye shall eat among all the beasts that are on the earth. Whatsoever parteth the hoof, and is clovenfooted, and cheweth the cud, among the beasts, that shall ye eat." These laws serve to set disciples apart from surrounding nations and to promote health and cleanliness. Clean animals include cattle, sheep, and goats, while unclean animals include pigs, shellfish, and certain birds.

The Law of Sacrifice

The law of sacrifice is central to the Old Testament, outlining the various offerings made to God for atonement and thanksgiving. Leviticus 1-7 describes different types of sacrifices, such as burnt offerings, sin offerings, and peace offerings. These sacrifices were a way for the Israelites to maintain a right relationship with God and to seek forgiveness for sins. However, these sacrifices were ultimately fulfilled in Jesus Christ, whose sacrifice on the cross made the need for animal sacrifices obsolete. Hebrews 10:10 states, "By the which will we are sanctified through the offering of the body of Jesus Christ once for all."

Perpetual Covenants

Many of God's laws, including the observance of the Sabbath and various feasts, are described as perpetual covenants. For example, Exodus 31:16 states,

"Wherefore the children of Israel shall keep the sabbath, to observe the sabbath throughout their generations, for a perpetual covenant." These perpetual laws are intended to last forever, underscoring their ongoing relevance and importance. They are a reminder of God's unchanging nature and His everlasting covenant with His people.

Jesus and the Fulfillment of the Law

Jesus' arrival marked the fulfillment of the law, not its abolition. In Matthew 5:17, Jesus declares, "Think not that I am come to destroy the law, or the prophets: I am not come to destroy, but to fulfil." Jesus upheld the moral law, embodied the ceremonial law, and transcended the civil law, demonstrating that the heart of the law is love for God and neighbor. Through His life, death, and resurrection, Jesus fulfilled the sacrificial system, providing a way for humanity to be reconciled with God.

While Jesus fulfilled the law and emphasized its spirit over its letter, He also provided a stricter and more profound interpretation of certain laws, revealing their deeper moral and ethical dimensions. In the Sermon on the Mount, Jesus expands on several commandments, calling His followers to a higher standard of righteousness. For instance, in Matthew 5:21-22, He states, "Ye have heard that it was said of them of old time, Thou shalt not kill; and whosoever shall kill shall be in danger of the judgment: But I say unto you, That whosoever is angry with his brother without a cause shall be in danger of the judgment." Here, Jesus teaches that not only is the physical act of murder sinful, but harboring anger and hatred in one's heart is equally condemnable. This interpretation demands a transformation of inner attitudes, not just outward compliance.

Similarly, Jesus addresses the commandment against adultery, intensifying its implications. In Matthew 5:27-28, He declares, "Ye have heard that it was said by them of old time, Thou shalt not commit adultery: But I say unto you, That whosoever looketh on a woman to lust after her hath committed adultery with her already in his heart." By extending the sin of adultery to include lustful thoughts, Jesus underscores the importance of purity and fidelity at the heart level, beyond mere external actions. These teachings highlight that true obedience to God's laws involves a holistic and sincere devotion that encompasses both our actions and our inner thoughts and desires. Christ's stricter interpretations reveal that His followers are called to a deeper, more comprehensive standard of righteousness that reflects the holiness and perfection of God Himself.

The Law and the New Covenant

Under the New Covenant, disciples are called to live by the spirit of the law rather than its letter. Romans 8:2 states, "For the law of the Spirit of life in Christ Jesus hath made me free from the law of sin and death." The New Covenant emphasizes internal transformation and a personal relationship with God, guided by the Holy Spirit. The principles of God's laws remain, but the law of sacrifice find fulfillment in Christ, who is the perfect sacrifice, the lamb of God.

Living in Obedience

Living in obedience to God's laws is a hallmark of a faithful disciple. James 1:22 exhorts disciples, "But be ye doers of the word, and not hearers only, deceiving your own selves." Obedience to God's laws is not about legalism but about expressing love for God and others, seeking to reflect God's holiness in every aspect of life. It involves understanding the heart of the law and applying its principles in ways that honor God and serve humanity.

Conclusion

God's laws, encompassing moral, ceremonial, civil, and dietary instructions, provide a comprehensive guide for living a life that pleases Him. While the Old Testament laws set the foundation, Jesus Christ fulfilled and expanded their meaning under the New Covenant. Understanding and adhering to God's laws involves a heartfelt commitment to holiness, justice, and love,

A Prayer for the Disciples of Christ

Heavenly Father,

We come before You with hearts full of gratitude and reverence for the calling You have placed on our lives as disciples of Christ. Lord, we thank You for the gift of salvation through Your Son, Jesus, and for the guidance of the Holy Spirit who leads us in truth and righteousness. We ask for Your strength and wisdom as we strive to follow Jesus' example in our daily lives.

Help us, Father, to walk in love, joy, peace, patience, kindness, goodness, faithfulness, gentleness, and self-control, reflecting the fruit of the Spirit in all we do. May our lives be a testament to Your grace and mercy, drawing others to the light of Christ. Equip us with courage and boldness to proclaim the gospel, to serve others selflessly, and to stand firm in our faith amidst trials and challenges.

Lord, unite us as a community of disciples, bound together by Your love. Teach us to support and encourage one another, to bear each other's burdens, and to grow together in faith and maturity. May our fellowship be a source of strength and joy, nurturing our spirits and spurring us on to good works.

We surrender our lives to Your will, O God. Use us for Your glory and the advancement of Your kingdom. Let our hearts be ever faithful, our minds ever focused on Your Word, and our actions ever reflective of Your love. In the name of Jesus Christ, our redeemer, we pray.

Amen